you are perfect!

you are perfect!

you are perfect!

You inspire me every day

You inspire me every day

see the
beauty here

see the
beauty here

see the
beauty here

I'M PROUD
OF YOU

I'M PROUD
OF YOU

I'M PROUD OF YOU

find a
reason to
smile

find a
reason to
smile

find a
reason to
smile

Take the scenic route

Delete the
entire recipe

Take the scenic route

i've always known it was you

i've always
known it
was you

i've always always known it was you

TODAY IS
YOUR DAY

TODAY IS

YOUR DAY

TODAY IS YOUR DAY

follow
your bliss

follow
your bliss

follow
your bliss

This is the right way

This is the

right way

This is the right way

you
totally made
my day

you

totally made

my day

you
totally made
my day

DREAM BIG

AND SMALL

five!

rigid

live!

high five!

Spread the love

Spread
the love

here is good

here is good

here is good

DREAM BIG

AND SMALL

DREAM BIG

AND SMALL

BE WHO YOU WANT TO BE

BE WHO YOU WANT TO BE